Home Movies of Narcissus

Camino del Sol

A Latina & Latino Literary Series

The University of Arizona Press

Home Movies of Narcissus

poems by Rane Arroyo

Tucson

Dedicated to Anita Josefina, yet another ghost in Ohio
to Glenn and Little Bee

The University of Arizona Press
© 2002 Rane Arroyo
All rights reserved. First Printing.

07   06   05   04   03   02   6   5   4   3   2   1

Copyright and CIP data can be found on page 76.

De buscar a Narciso fatigada
sin permitir sosiego a mi pie erranta.
[Worn out with searching for Narcissus, granting
my wandering foot no respite.]

—Sor Juana, *The Divine Narcissus*

Contents

Some of these poems were previously published—often under different titles and in earlier versions. Many thanks to the editors and readers of *Argestes, Architrave, Bakunin, Barrow Street, Behind Bars, Contraband, Farmer's Market, Field, Gyst, Gerbil, The Heartlands Today: Cultural Quilt, The Heartlands Today: Characters & Voices, Heliotrope, Horizontes: Revista Hispanica, Louisville Review, Many Mountains Moving, Mockingbird, Poems & Plays, RiverSedge, Snakeskin,* and *Whirligig.*

In addition, "The Body Shop," "Dream Starring Andy Garcia," and "That Flag" are from *The Naked Thief,* which won the 1997 Stonewall National Chapbook Competition. Gracias to Clarinda Harris and David Bergman and their intelligent hearts.

"A Bolero, but Not for Dancing" was presented at a Modern Language Association's Performance Theory Panel under the conference title, "Salsa Capitalism: The Story of Juan Angel."

"Happy Birthday Me," "Three Easters without Sugar," and "Two-Headed Piñata" were published in the chapbook *Weekends in Ohio with Ghosts* (Last Minute Press, 2000). Thanks to Eric Bekoe, Erica Feingold, Linda Floyd, and Jeffrey Runokivi.

An early version of "The Ponce de León Poems" was published in its entirety in *The Caribbean Writer.* Research for this poem was sponsored by a grant from The University of Toledo's College of Arts and Sciences.

"Spanish Lessons" was published in the anthology *Learning by Heart,* edited by Maggie Anderson and David Hassler (University of Iowa Press, 1999).

Acknowledgments

Home Movies of Narcissus

1 Yes, Sí, Aha

Some Faces

Wearing this shaving cream mask,
I work towards a shining.
Later, I tell you in the bar,
Tierra Nueva: "Every brother
to his beard of beer foam!"
Youth loves to say yes, *sí*, aha.

.

I pass a mirror, look at myself:
nude in a large net of light.
A mustache would disguise me
but why bother, for morning
always finds me, calls me by name.
Hijo, I call myself, son of the sun.

.

My morning beard signifies
that something happened
to me last night: midnight?
love? what? no souvenirs?
I wear my father's face in
a city older than my heart.

Spanish Lessons

Today's word: *agua*.
Water, like in your
mother's womb. Water,
like in the river through
Jayuya, Puerto Rico.
Water insists there be
thirst in the world and
that thirst is the source
of all songs. Yesterday's
word: *amarillo*. The word
in Spanish has the "y"
sound as in yellow and
not the "l" sound as in
Amarillo, Texas. Tomorrow's
word: *arroz*. Rice is linked
conceptually to arroyo,
or dry river. They both
need agua to exist. How
the dead thirst for this world.
It takes so much water to grow
rice! I never understood
any teacher's flat tone of
voice when speaking of facts.
Language is music's twin.
Newspapers confused me also:
arroz stopped growing in
wet Vietnam even as
the Arroyos grew in Chicago.

My Childhood Home

Addresses that add up to 3 are dizzy, but spiritual.
—Radio Numerologist

We had guests working
toward wrinkled clothes
on the living room dance floor,
salvation beyond slavish paychecks.

The bathtub was ground zero,
bed of ice and floating bottles.
I was called *The Professor*
for hiding books in my pockets

while I twisted and shouted with
the young uncles begging rum
for blood transfusions, for fevers.
We weren't afraid of God—then.

Dream of My Vanished Father

He smashes the side door with
a neighbor's golf club. Throws
the boxes of eggs into the basement.
This puzzles the lawyers in

the frowning courtroom the most.
Freed on bond, he changes
to black clothes in the rest area
next to the airplane museum.

Geese pass by bearing stars.
Dancers with huge heads
ask to borrow pants and a lace
tablecloth, but he is poorer

than even the stars. He returns
home only to find a nun scrubbing
his dulled pillows. Avoiding her
handshake, he steps on a lonely nail.

Father looks like the child I'll never make.
Where is the Christ of his childhood,
he who would play hide and seek
in the mouths of dumb crocodiles?

Vanishing Cousin

Another cousin done in
ways that no all-male porno
can make glamorous:
heroin body hair.

.

Goddamn the Pusherman
was the song we listened to
through hard headphones,
those strange stethoscopes.

.

We would rent bathing suits
and how different our bodies were,
though as cousins we shared
the same angry blood.

.

"Semen is white and not golden
like the sun."
"Are you sure?
How can we each hide a waterfall?"

.

I've diagnosed us since as
suffering with Ponce de León
Fever. The new world is never
new to our ancient erections.

·

My body is my best friend.
Once, cousin, you were that
as we burned up the map of
Europe with Indian-red crayons.

·

You're nervous at being quoted:
*Sad, no? The way we have to bring
our bones on all our travels
and how God owns our asses?*

The Cousins

We're drunk, telling the old
stories of life on George Street,
when a cha-cha-cha Chicago
used to be ours. We threw
stones at chance cars to prove
we weren't our scared elders.

How we hid from the angry
ghost-colored drivers and our
tropics-starved parents under
the houses of mutual silences.
One, whose weighty mother
put a red high heel through his

"too-thin skull," would lick ants
to gross us out. He did get to us.
Another showed us what Zorro's
erection should look like; nothing
new. We invented our own game:
What's in the addict's attic?

The past doesn't embrace applause.
We ran toward mambo manhood,
not understanding that we couldn't
escape it. Some of us are in educating
jails, others in dumb marriages.
I'm doing this, whatever this is.

Delicious Parable

Here we are at a convenience store
with one row of Puerto Rican
products and my mother crosses
herself. Nothing has prices, but
we fill up baskets with yautia,
plátanos, and other edible maps.
Mother rushes and grabs the bacalao,
dried codfish. Tasty skeleton of salt,
it's the gilled grail, Neptune's diary.
Mother acts as if we're both jewelers
as the clerk weighs our goods—for
they are good. How much a pound?
Expensive, pensively so, OK, *sí*.
We drive back through ghettos in
which children don't play. Or eat?
The poor no longer have children, Mami,
and she nods—not listening for she's
planning tomorrow's meal. I cry
later at home, for this food is
the only inheritance she can give me,
this meal with chance bones in it.

Three Easters without Sugar

Beginning in wisdom, dying in doubt
—Robert Lowell, "Tenth Muse"

Tío, what do ghosts eat and
why do memories make me hungry?
I ache on seeing three plantains
ripening on the red windowsill:
the peasant food on which we
were raised. Verdad, Uncle, I'm
turning into Narcissus's stunt double.

.

Tío, I've no Aretha Franklin
to offer you, no champagne. Gulped by
god, you haven't met my new cats yet.
Have you RSVP'd your resurrection?
I set off another cockroach bomb.
Isn't resurrection what insects
do best: egg after egg after egg?

.

Tío, did you take up the shape
of a burning bird that banged
against the clear window of a New
England bed-and-breakfast in which
I touched my latest award—as if braille?
Or are you just dust? My latest tears
turn you into a monument of mud.

Young in the Heartland

We're anatomically correct
romantics running through cornfields
higher than Christ's thorned head at

the High Street Church. We lose our
slow clothing, but it's OK because
we're not secrets. Let us become

the landscape: Adam dressed in corn silk,
Icarus in his ancient cockpit.
Scarecrows call out, *hermanos!*

Dream Starring Andy Garcia

He walked naked into
the party, put his
head on my hard lap,
wept because he
didn't have a shadow.
Talk turned to Greek
statues. He asked why
his morning beard was
black while his pubic hair
was red. I pushed him
into the shower. He
pulled me in and I
also wept with him
at not having a God
in any of my images.
The party dragged us
back into its endless
singing of "Happy Birthday"
to the sun. I stayed
in this dream until
9:45 A.M. when a beer truck
on Temple Street blew
its horn. Happiness
is so easily stolen.

Happy Birthday Me

Happy Birthday me, I sing
as a thunderstorm blurs by.

The weatherman explains
that this storm will extinguish

itself in a Canada plagued
by snow. It's a small birthday

party of one, even as twelve die
from black rains in Puerto Rico.

Dancing alone in a haunted city
owned by fat landlords who can

afford to kick me and cats out,
it's another weekend with ghosts.

If the lights do go out, there are
candles on my cake. This storm must

soon tire into tiny teardrops. I wish
that all of us exiles finally unpack.

Death of a Poet's Cat

My dying cat loves when
I type a poem. To her it's music.
Am I of sound mind?

I'm over twenty years late
in my turn at a conversation
with a kilt-wearing professor:

"I think Wordsworth is more
interesting as an old man.
When one's pubic hairs go

gray, miracles promise secret
logic." Revolutions burn
down houses, which will not

stay ash. The Void gets bored.
My cat sleeps, her face towards
the false dawn of my desk lamp.

It's all I can offer her. She has
been there for all my poems for
the last five years. "Kitty

Dialysis" is what Glenn says we do.
It's the opposite of the teat:
shots in the morning, liquids

throughout the day. She shows up
in my dreams with telepathic

15

whiskers. It's why Wordsworth's

"Excursion" makes me sad, abstract
ruin without tourists or T-shirts.
He writes of "faith become / a passionate

intuition." He's 44, the same age I am
for one more month. Time, stay overnight.
Anita, I don't need an angel, por favor.

Proof

A coffee cup shatters,
an heirloom's shards.
My shaking hands,
unshakable life lines.
I'm growing a goatee,
a mask. Itchy eye,
the devil's crap table.
I re-read Neruda to stay
awake. Vast sky in
the new living room
window. Ambitious
nights are bound to find
my latest aging address.
I sweep up this last
proof of my childhood:
silly cup with mock windmill.
What need was there for
a lullaby with prophecy
attached: *Que será, será?*
I can't deny this sorrow, this
loss. Was I ever a child?

II   The Mask Museum

Bad Disguises

Who shall I be this Halloween?
Leashed Antonio Banderas in

a Hollywood-scripted codpiece?
If only I could hire the young Picasso

as a special effects consultant.
Richard Nixons, Joe McCarthys, and

Andrew Carnegies scream "Treat!"
at my door. I've my soul to offer.

Capitalism's sweet tooth
will be legendary when we're extinct.

Am I Quixote on crack?
Someone in a devil's mask

demands my green card. It's a joke,
but not for me. When is this home?

The Body Shop

Augusto knows his sex
wants a diary of its
own. His pet—an unfixed
racing car—is good bad

company. He stopped
going to church after
thinking that some of
Noah's wet dreams couldn't

have been prophecies.
Beauty shows up in
Augusto's body
shop as the Mustang that

got away. Stranded in
his own life, he hot-wires
bottles of rum until
he's not ugly to

himself. Augusto sits
in his racing car and
blasts out love songs.
He knows all the words.

Unfunded Art

The unclothed models in
Santana's studio
let their bodies tell of
explicit lives: gunshot
craters, gang tattoos.
These nudes are our prayers
with their stone testicles,
full-moon breasts, coronas
of hair. They contradict
pouty Narcissus by
loving their beauty
long before losing it.

Red Wine with Roberto

A socialite wants the government
to open up brothels to close the legs
of strangers in parks. Why should her

city be safer than mine? I want
to want, to skinny-dip inside my
television, to eat off the blue hands

of matadors, to betray my dead
husband like some Spider Woman,
Eva Perón, María Magdalena,

a Hollywood spitfire, a hot tamale,
a very dark lady. I like imagining
strangers having sex in this dying

city, giving mouth to mouth in these
tragic times. It makes Eden seem
real, possible, just blocks from here.

I Killed Zorro

Masked men are magnets.
Does he stuff his hero pants?
Is New Spain aging badly?
As a public citizen, Zorro's

sword is the last word.
Handsome icon maker, his
Z is language as summary.
For verbs, there is his horse.

Caped ones are all the angels
most of us will ever know.
What can we offer to the fox
with clean nails and shining boots

in seasons of mud? He is bubble butt
theater in tight pants, his mustache
as precise as God's signature.
In unmasking him, I will prove

the wealthy need to own
everything, that our hearts
are always their hidden empires.
In unmasking him, I'll be godless.

Miss Lola Plans Her Funeral

1. About the Wake

It should be a simple affair, or not.
Why be humble when worms brag of their guts?

No classical music; never tame beasts.
My soul's old barn is empty. Help the priest

be drunk. I love his knock knock jokes. Hire
some kids with a garage band. Their fire

will be cheap fireworks. *Don't* invite Don,
Little Julie, Marilyn Hayworth, Grand

Steve, or Krazy Karlos and his boy, Pearl.
They're too ugly to exist in the world,

while it's mine. What to wear? Depends on what
I die of. No blue, if I drown. No hat

if I fall off a skyscraper. No red
if I check out in a cheap hotel bed.

I'll choose five outfits. No new shoes—they pinch.
(I'm walking to Eternity, that inch.)

2. Shopping for Her Casket

Peapod, giant lipstick case, big bullet—
It's shaped like a turd and just as brilliant.

The names: Rockabye, God's Nest, Beyond Blue.
Sans seat belts, condoms, exit doors, old views.

Make mine plain: deny Michelangelo.
I'll wear an adolescent's face, a cello's.

3. Instructing Father Rodrigo on His Funeral Speech

I saw Our Lady once at a bar and
she waved to me with such a hairy hand.

One long night, I woke up in a cell next to
a runaway whose stiletto heels knew

too much of Kingdom Come. Mention how thin
I was during the Reagan years. No sins

matter when one looks fabulous, like you
in that ancient black dress heavy with truths.

But you know I praise you, our own Heathcliff!
Use your bass voice, love—offer hieroglyphs.

4. Selecting the Burial Site

Not near a tree. All that bird shit falling
like comets. And of course, there's that singing—

I'd never get my beauty rest. No, not
near the highway. I'd envy those wheeled yachts

roaring past while I drowned in my stillness.
Not next to these hairless angels whose chests

prove their sculptors knew nothing of the heart.
This endless sea of grass has no lifeguard.

Here, or there, or better yet—surprise me.
I won't blame you; I'll sue Eternity.

This is a launching pad, a mock mailbox,
resurrection's address book, a hatbox.

I'm no Jimmy Morrison worshipped in
Paris: his tomb like a teenage wet dream:

condoms, joints, beer cans, bad poems, scraps of
shopping lists. Only the doomed are that loved.

That's nice: a hill, hell in a grass skirt, lump
in God's throat, home sweet home in Dante's rump.

The Poet's Body

to Boris Pasternak

The poet's body is more
than a body; it is
the space between

ceiling and floor,
house and space,
planet and nothing.

His or her shadows
are black, the color
of the cosmos when

alone with itself.
The four walls of his
or her lifetime make

claims to the poet's
breaths later, years
later. Echoes can be

heard of the body
and the mind at war.
Stop, says the poet,

tears in his or her eyes,
*for I'm becoming too
real. There's a spear*

plunged in someone
else's savior's side.
Why does it also hurt me?

A Bolero, but Not for Dancing

Cecilia sits in the darkening living room in Puerto Rico. Her brother's male lover has come to tell of Juan Angel's funeral. Cecilia talks to make the meeting important, an event to remember.

What I dislike about daylight is its
muscularity. What need to claim
everything, only to release it
at dusk, when man and woman need a
godparent? Do you notice how my
hands seem blue and yet I'm wearing no
sapphire nor do I play the piano?
I'm the last in my family to go
gray, but what talent lies in that claim?
I do fly—in dreams in which I'm not
in Santurce, but on Saturn, or in
a Venice not yet painted by a
Puerto Rican. Curiosity
may well prove to be a domestic art.
If you notice, I live alone, although
so do the sun and moon, but then they
share the same sky, small purple spaces
in my eyes. My desires I've tamed
because of experience: Orion
never does grow naked, the Big
Dipper never solves anyone's thirst
on Earth. From inside my house, this planet
seems flat, a matter of walls to knock
down or build doors into, or from which
to hang photos. That's Juan Angel
on the beach on the night of some saint.

Lord Byron, perhaps. No, that's a joke.
Juan called me his Sor Juana and I
did cry. I was forbidden to read as a
young girl. Knowledge was too unstable
a dowry. My brother was beautiful.
But you've seen him. You may know that
better than I do. But still, the white trunks,
the moonlight, the white foam of a wave
bound to break against him, light from
some galaxy in the sky—Sirius,
perhaps—sí, Sirius howling
overhead. See how a glass frame turns my
Juan Angel into a classical ghost.
There are mirrors and there are masks,
and there are always masks in the mirror.
It's easy to misquote the dead, no?
Now: only there is no now. Rum at least
lies to one. You must have driven blindly
down back roads of the grief that brought you
to me. Do I disappoint you with
my plainness? I'm not a tourist site.
Once, conversations threatened to pull this
house apart, nail by nail, plank by plank,
but then once Juan Angel was alive.
He chose never to visit me because
then he couldn't be an orphan.
He never realized that I became one,
too. I bought a parrot. At his death,
my brother's, and not the parrot's, though both
are dead, I got dressed in my leather
coat—unusual in my Puerto Rico,
but that's the point. I went to see

the mummified remains of the island's
Vatican-approved St. Pío, who
had been young, once. What remains is
the idea of his form, under the
bandages, below the glass coffin that
makes the saint seem a snob. So I left
my fingerprints all over the church
and cried for Juan Angel en el Parque
de Campanas, near a jail, a different
kind of church. You and I share similar
desires, not that most human
desires are very different from
each other. Except for serial killers
and Buddhist priests, both groups prizing
nothingness, abstinence of pleasure.
At least my priests are in constant and
perhaps eternal pain. And not over
love. But lust. It's the force that helped the
Barbarians batter the doors of
Roman empires. But that's not why I
have dead bolts. No, I have many dead.
I sat under the ordinary eyes of pigeons
without any bread to offer them and
I thought about the prisoners—in
cells at the bottom of that cliff. Naked
before God. I imagined them as
sailors forced into the fortresses
of their solitary natures. My
hand reached out for their visibility.
I walked towards the jail and looked down.
One man looked up and grabbed his crotch. .
For me, it was a seashell grabbed from

the Aegean, a collect call from Neptune,
a blue rose from Atlantis, an eel
to cook in my famous garlic sauce.
Then the poor young boy left the yard and
entered hell, only without a Dante.
Oh, I know literature. Juan Angel
read it to me aloud because
growing up there was no pornography.
One just acted it out. I caught a dark
taxi away from that park and went to
an American bar. But I didn't look or
drink like a fallen or falling woman.
I don't own a radio. I used to have many
records, a great name for the music
that accompanies us. To break a record. To
record thoughts. I have some left. My second
lover gave me this bolero. He
was an athlete. Your height but, I think, more
hung. I make you blush? Enjoy a rose,
when you can. Was Juan Angel beautiful
and aggressive? Those two traits don't always
go together. Consider dolphins.
Beautiful but so dependent on the skirts
of cruise ships that pass through the blue
purgatory of the tropical peace.
I know that you were his . . . friend. Have I
tired you out? Is that in my power?
I'm sure he would comfort you now only
he is the one lost in true time itself.
I keep on breathing. I've walked around this
house so many times that my steps are
maps. But I hurt you by calling him

by name. Your smile is either a dismissal
or an admission. In either case,
it proves you've listened to me. You know
what you know, but not what I know. That
will never be yours. Amusing oneself
after 40 becomes an art. Art becomes
less and less about male statues coming
to life and stepping into white, tight gift
underwear from the moon. It's about
playing one song over and over
again, and learning how to stop weeping.
It's about one goddamn song in your
goddamn mind and how it's goddamn new
with each goddamn hearing. Nothing is
ever in our control. It is time for you
to leave, while you can, while the ghosts
under the palm trees are busy eating
each other, while sharks jump from roof to
roof to see if stars are the real surface
of the sea, while a taxi can be found
to take you back into your grief,
a different monster than mine. The sad
part, my friend, is that you will return
to your photographs of Juan Angel
and I'll have this simple one: Juan Angel
as a merman, clasped not in Abraham's
bosom but Neptune's, or a dead sailor's,
or Hart Crane's perhaps. See how we mourn
two different men? We are almost allies.

Cecilia locks the door after Nestor and shuts off all the lights of the
house. She watches her visitor disappear into the moonlight. She goes

through her jewelry box and finds nothing that seems right for the occasion for dreaming.

Gustavo's Saturday Night

Tonight, I'm in leather
and bare-knuckle cologne.
At the all-night Enchilada
Palace, I realize that
this is not an age in which

Shelley can be quoted
without someone smiling.
Darkness is always fashionable.
Back on the streets, my legs
blur into a river. The skyline

is a heartache turned away,
daring me to speak first.
Go slow, Romeo's friends
told him often. More advice:
not every city is God's.

Papo Auditions for the Role of Romeo

I've been in love, Sir. I've
borrowed a bed from a priest even
(don't ask, don't tell). Hell has

to be crowded with Playboy
bunnies and their poachers, no?
My Juliet must offer my true

codpiece its own bold wings
for Love is anti-gravity.
Romeo feeds on clouds and

gets drunk on vintage starlight.
There had to be a trapdoor in
his coffin. I know God's

got bloodhounds—but me and
Juliet, we'll hide out at a rave.
And Sir, I can become a blonde.

The Translator

He sits in San Juan, his sidereal back
to the sea, his spine's compass shining with

directions to *here*. He is no tourist,
no transverse wave scouting for the cosmos,

no aesthete of tanning. A need for
purpose shapes the transonic skyline of

his labors, a city of his editing and humming.
It's noon, that wounded light unarmed before

the venery at the beach. He has to bring
his own darkness to the table, and does so.

Searching for home by thinking inside it
(an ancient strategy), he asks the volcano

how it increases itself from within.
It's been years since he has felt joy, or

joy has possessed him—years without toucans.
It feels good to be at a café and not in

his kolkhoz of a room. He feels safer
among the laughing, safer questioning

comets before witnesses. The King's English
contrasts with the Spanish of his dreams, a fluency

in bad beds. He writes slowly. Translating
is always washing someone else's heir.

The waiters mistake his despair as complaints.
They rush glasses of bold wine to his table.

In the mirroring bar, he is the mask museum.
The pages of his wages are notes turned

into mobs. Each poem is an imbroglio,
a brittle bomb. He has no words of his own.

III Hungry Ghost

The Ponce de León Poems

1　I, Ponce de León, Return to Our World

. . . and the miracle of the sea still stirs
my stilled skull. New light bursts from
my dark solar plexus. I'm back *home*
to the land haloed by human breath.
Alive again, I'm wounded, my old islands
now have skyscrapers instead of palm trees.
The statues to me are unsung and gray with
years shunned by shock-proof tourists.
My poor hysterical Hispañola is
unhusbanded without me; Puerto Rico
turns *pobre*. I'm their red-haired hurricane
returned to economies of false starts.
Has that far fountain been found yet?
Am I old alone? How crowded these islands.
Something shakes me, something like a bell.
I'm seized, but not by a seizure. History
was easy once: a wave of my young sword
as I rode waves towards the craved kingdom
of the Eye. It was all mine to claim.
Hunger is still all I know of forever.
I'm no one's souvenir—but God's.
But not yet. Anonymity is the worm
that eats body and soul long after
burial, a deep sleep in real space.
To be forgotten is a daily death.
The sea has taught my spirit how to leash
a volcano and ride it towards cold light.
I must find a poet to haunt, someone
to help me forever flee the footnote.

2   The Poet Rejects Ponce de León's Offer to Be a Muse

Sorry, Señor de Sorrows,
but I'm not the poet who
will write you a winged
epic, so grow bald
in that hairy grave.
A rum fiesta
is down the red
street: sunset. I still
live here, my here.
And, no, I'm not your
pet cockatoo. Your
mad rule over
stolen land is
over, and as for myth:
no fountain, no
gain. Gracias for
the passé anger,
but the dead are
always generous
with useless gifts.
We are wealthy with
our plastic surgeons,
plastic flatware,
plastic flamingoes,
plastic card calypsos.
Ponce, we've improvised
your unfound fountain.
Some other writer
must need you, amigo,
a CyberLowRider,

a CosmiVaquero,
any CatholicSka
(a monk in dreads).
Leave me, Señor.
Seduce someone else with
fame or infamy.
The age of the epic
is gone, Governor,
and statues are
now abstract, story-free.
—Well, one poem then,
a catered exorcism,
a bon voyage for old bones.
Then *adios*, Conqueror.

3 Promised Poem:
Being Ponce de León

The nobles among the sailors
use handkerchiefs
on their bloody noses.
The common sailors
wash their faces in the sea.
Under a Catholic God,
Ponce de León sneezes in
private. His holy breath
strains the starving sails.
He drinks wine, red as
the ruby fields reported
in India's riverbeds.
He walks naked under
the man-in-the-moon's scowl,
asks the drowned, "Which
God claims your clatter?"
To calm himself down, Ponce
demands a civilizing shave:
23 servants spy on him
through narrow doors.
They mock his balding head,
comment that it's shaped like
a bony fist and that roses
in new worlds decay like
those in gardens left behind.
More wine is brought.
Some spills onto maps,
future trails of blood.

4 I, Ponce de León, Protest the Age of the Lyric

This poet is a clumsy ventriloquist
and this is what he publishes,
the bastard. I've killed for much less.
Arroyo is an amateur
magician; where are the maffick rhymes?
Jewels without cuts are only stones;
stones without shine are the skulls of stars.
Any lyric is a terrible lie
(it's the law of that form). This is his
pathetic séance, a mere brief aside.
What's up and down with that? That poem?
As monument to me? That black eye?
This poet has a piñata for a heart.
Learn, hijito—the accent mark
over the hard word "León" is
a savage knife falling from Heaven.

5 Promised Poem, Second Attempt:
The Young Ponce de León

VOICES:
Numbers. Numbers.

PONCE'S FATHER:
My son is from and part
of the first family in Spain to join
Queen Isabella's crusade to turn us
into a giant who feeds on blood.

A NEIGHBOR:
He is just one of twenty-one sins against
the Holy Ghost, songs of misspent semen.
Twenty-one lions loose in old Spain.
Twenty-one Spains before one lion?

VOICES:
Numbers. Numbers.

A SOLDIER:
He wars at the age of fourteen.
Other boys' fathers rot in this aged land.
He gives neither Heaven nor Hell hostages.
Hero by denying the zero in his bones.

A NUN:
Zero is the number we stole from The
Sahara. It's heterotopic in
our excesses of spiritual censure.
Zero shares the egg's shape, eyeballs, balls.

45

VOICES:
Numbers. Numbers.

COLUMBUS:
Zero flowers in the new world, home to
birds and ghosts—interchangeable species.

PONCE'S MOTHER:
The three-in-one god's ten commandments seem
to limit Juan Ponce de León to
vices older than his age, but this rage
is aged wine, Satan's own victualer.

VOICES:
Numbers. Numbers.

PONCE:
A sum summarizes a summons.
The whole always hides holes, whore
with greater belief in the unending
to come than have comet readers or court
eunuchs. I am my own meaning.

6   I, Ponce de León, Am Not Jealous of El Cid

Ahh, what do they teach you in those
English-language prisons? If the moon
drops diamonds without remorse, why not you?
Pero tienes miedo, hijo. Such fear.
Arroyo, replace light's windows
with tapestries. Opacity
is the heavy city of Jerusalem
crowded with Crusaders spending
their curt blood. My words, your mouth:
an ancient trade route. Transformation
is just a braggart. The old is old.
A witch of San Terva said to put
rags of roses in my mouth when
I was born: hunger. Then chickens were
sacrificed, cleaned, cooked because of my red
hair; I was the sun's bastard, wearing
my mother's burning blood inside and out.
Then the Moor wars, then I was a cocksman.
I steered my promiscuity until I was
a mast in a new world: "Follow a mermaid,"
I said to the enslaved compass.
Then the salty empire of my labor.
Too much now, too much then. Ships can burn
on water, know that? Learn that fever is both
the message and the messenger.
Write me a defense that distracts from facts.
The fountain between my legs, poeta,
that was history, el futuro, *el futuro.*

7   The Poet Shakes Off Ponce de León's Hungry Ghost

Morning wakes up wearing
the holy underwear of snow.
The ventriloquist's séance
last night was a bust. No ghost
from a nearby star joins me
for coffee from Thailand, land
my speech therapist insists
I don't pronounce as Thigh-Land.
Gold roses the size of baby fists
make me think of Florida when
it flowered before being forced
to wear weary Eden's fig leaf.
X used to call our lovemaking
a ménage, which sounds like
a Dutch Elm disease. That's what
you get, Héctor told me long ago,
for having an imagination.
I was young a few hairstyles ago.
I'm back to my instant breakfast
and notebooks rotting like apples.

8   The Poet's Nightmare with Cameo by Ponce de León

The terrible Taino shows me his
wounds, and I put my hand
in the one near his heart. Cold,
the black hole there, a cold
not of the tropics. I am
accused of praising him,
Ponce de León, the cross's
claw, the blood lover.
Then a hailstorm of heads of
Christianized slaves,
and each one cries out: Write
of us who are buried
without tombstones far from
our mourners. I weep
because salt is an honest
gift that is ours to give:
Heaven, see my beard of tears.
A black moon mocks me.

PONCE DE LEÒN INTERRUPTS:
We all speak sorrow, son.
It's the language of history.

9   The Exhausted Poet

To be young forever
is one way to overthrow
any of the graying gods.
But research what?
Untranslated papers
mispronounce the lost moments
of a man, a ship, a fountain.
He died on a far Cuba,
paradise become a casket.
One spring, I went to the cathedral
named for him and strangers
asked me to be a godfather
to their red son. "The rain
has caused delays and we believe Satan
wants the soul of our heir."
Where is that child? Where am I?
Ponce is also the pouting name
of a city in Puerto Rico, but
its beautiful and famous fire station
can't cool this fever. I map
a lover for I've fate lines to deny.
The bedsheets are blank sheets of paper.
Ponce's ghost is lost! At last!
Noon, your big yellow is simple,
a bee's brain. I'm naked,
no Sunday paper. We hold on
to Saturday, laughing
that my silly erection
is an 11th finger, one that

wants either a wedding ring
or flea collar. I'll write these
Ponce de León poems later,
when I'm old. Delirious,
the cat wants out, out there.
The radio: *oh, baby, it's a wild
world*. Like God's mind?

10   I, Ponce de León, Declare War on Poets

You are all memorialists with
nothing to confess. Narcissus,
at least, had his eyes open, and
that damming pool was of this world.
As black-clad black holes, poets
steal breaths of days meant to be
misspent, miserable, mislaid.
And for what? To excuse their drinking?
I will now haunt a historian, kinder
fabulist. Arroyo, I kick you to the curb—
and take your hipped Ricky Martin with you.
Puertorriqueños, you have forgotten
that Old Spain is your Mother who
demands blood, those liquid rubies.
We bribed the Gods we could, killed
the others. Poetry should praise scars.

My island is as theatrical as
any sleepwalker's house. Your biblical
dependency on a fisherman explains
the hooks in your mouth, mouths. Unzipped, you
are the sun's zealot. That remains true. Beds
with tourists are never an escape route;
you are the foreigner in your own nights.
Midnight is my confidante, ever since
I was killed by an arrow, that plush *pling*,
a singing rush to a horizontal view of
the hardening ancient sky. Funny, how
softness is the dream now. Mine no saint's death:
no hot pokers up any of my known ports,
no cannibal's communion, no drowning
in my enemy's blood as did gilled Samson.
You are my zip coded heir, poor puppet.
Isla, forgive our Arroyo for his conquering
words and not worlds; poets can be used
to hide the bodies from historians and God.
Don't hurt through heroin, hype, or hoopla
of santería souvenir shopping. Don't hurt.
Priests have sold you to allies; know that
enemies are the best of all anchors.
Island of slow *sangre*, let others starve
their hearts; enjoy another feast on a
black tablecloth with pink silk-stitched stars,
the colors of old wounds. Your rain forest
veils overfed cities. Airports return
the coffins of your tired corpses, for cash.
Why isn't spectacle ever a condemnation?

But, sí, voting Republican can only lead
to blonde grandchildren, and see what good
they have done me? Turn coconuts into
milk nurses. Nothing wrong with stealing silver
from mirrors, but nothing brave about it.
Colonize the moonlight. Be worthy of love.

The young age in each
other's dramas. Birds in
dancing trees. The multi-
lingual are silent in
the arms of their desires.
The city receives runaways,
its economics based on
the harvest of thrown-away
names. Go-go dancers imitate
the sex aches of Praise, that
half-god without a purpose.
The aged are amazed by
what is whole. Open any
door and hurry into opulent
music. Murals give birth
to smiling suns who don't
seem too homesick for
the tropics. Chaos theoreticians
grow rich and bald. The young
are replaced by the younger.
Where are my honest ghosts?
What is a son without a father?
Statues keep predicting the wrong past.
Ponce? de León? Juan?

IV   The Black Moon Poems

The Book of Names

I was to be named Alejandro.
Poor Alex, what would have been

your story? Fate has the last word,
sticking its tongue in anyone's mouth

so we can't cry out: *Oh! My twin!*
I knew this loneliness was a false god!

Did that priest baptize all of my selves?
Once, the magnet was witchcraft.

Alex loves comparing scars. We laugh
as if birthing bells. Bunk beds

for us, drunk doppelgangers,
two wings hurrying nowhere.

I cannot imagine *not* being a poet,
being as anonymous as the wind.

News from the Country of Thought

I burn incense although I'm no priest
or a stoned prophet. I'm puzzled by
two wooden giraffes from Kenya that stare
at a broken clock. Naked lovers
tumble inside my TV, their told beds
as tiny earthquakes, just scripts of
gravity wrestling itself. I let these ideas
sink into their own dream skins.
The screen goes from flesh to total
eclipse. Outside, the first frost fixes
itself to dead flowers; it is that
hungry for form. I told a coke dealer
in a Beacon Hill S & M bar
that he was only selling the illusion
of snow, that the real thing is colder,
older, bolder. The biker's girlfriend
across the street is wearing falsies
again, looking like a pre-Stonewall
drag queen (Miss Candy Apple Red), but
see how happy she is wrapped about
her daredevil who is a leather dream.
I want a daydream like hers, as distracted
as that odd statue of an Aztec god in
Tijuana licking his red feet clean.
I'm condemned with condoms I never use.
Perhaps some body might be under me if
I could whisper in French or Russian,
but I want to learn stone-talk, dolphin-talk,
or tree-talk. Notebooks for firewood,
the room darkens to match my bones.
Soon, the black moon veils this page.

Night Ignores an SOS

Falling off a dream ladder,
I think of a new book to write:
The Glass Rags—or too
Pasolini crashing

a cranked frat party?
How dark my cooling limbs
against glowing bedsheets.
Why wear a morning beard at

midnight? No, a new title:
When Statues Bleed. Mozart
takes over the unloved radio,
chaos on its best behavior.

My bed is full of bad poems.
Gracias, Moon, I don't want to be
your food taster. The next book
must be named *Piñata Cowboys*.

People of the Piñata

I'm drunk while my parents
pray at midnight mass with
other people just as surprised

as they are to be old. I'm drunk
after a job interview that took
5 minutes; it took me one hour

to walk home in new begging shoes.
I'm drunk and toast a lost cousin
in jail whose sex life is "now so

very ambitious" while I stay home
to make *Art International* a meal.
I'm tasting rain on my lips from

a beer garden in a storm in which
a cousin came back from the dead;
gossip became manifestos.

I'm drunk, feeling political
like those transvestites in San Juan
who threw lit cigarettes at tourists

who mocked them in their own land.
I'm drunk and circle the piñata
shaped like a mule. I murder it.

Two-Headed Piñata

We have no family
cemetery, no future
address. The exiled
are doomed to be

leaves in the wind.
I'm any atheist's
prophet. The future
and the past are

a two-headed piñata
I cannot break. I try,
blow after blow,
to shatter these days,

for sweetness to reign.
It doesn't rain sugar.
Labor isn't always
salvation. Why isn't it?

Aching in Autumn

My dying cat is purring because
I'm home from a wedding reception

in which Christian women shook
their holy vessels after champagne.

Auden, you must be bored being dead.
My Anita Josefina looks out

of the black window into the black.
She will teach me to the very end:

In his home movies, Narcissus
is both the seen and the seer.

A Dark Rain

One more sleepless night. The newest translation
of Dante doesn't get me snoring. No Zs.
English, you love your letters: the ABCs,
T-shirts, the F-word, the N-word, V for

victory. Bananarama's "Cruel Summer"
vibrates in my brain stem, guest with tambourine.
It's a weekend to remember our dead;
the nation's ghosts are thrown wreaths of roses

as if lifesavers. A neighbor laughing—the frat boy
and not the retired soldier with oxygen mask
It's good that youth exists. It's bad that it's not
mine. Y is that? A for apple. I'm tired of

counting the suicides of Russian poets
in this era, in this ear. I wish to sit
in my underwear next to a drunk lover
looking at constellations on the white ceiling.

Transformation is a talent; for example:
the letter h is letters l and n mating.
Summer's first storm is here, a ripe darkness.
Thunder climbs down awkwardly from some distant

rage. Lightning takes off its stovepipe hat before
entering this emptying room. I'm packing
for a new life in a new city. B is
for boy, buoy, or bandages for a wound

that is my life. Three of these boxes are
manuscripts I'm to judge before June 15th.
Most titles are plain: *Bicycle in the Cemetery,*
Naked Shadows, Our Unpraised Seagulls.

Several of them have cranes: *My Lover the Crane,*
The Sorrows of Cranes, Cranes from Far Gods.
Wait! Lovers whisper under my front-yard tree,
a green umbrella I cannot take with me.

It's so dark now that I can't see the M in
either of my palms: M for *muerte,* the death
begun at birth. I love how humans hum with
energy so I'm truly troubled by Dante fainting

throughout purgatory. Poor Virgil,
a one-man ambulance, always having to
pretend astonishment at Dante's foolishness.
That lightning bit something north of here,

Thor's backyard! A heavy rain now, tears as
cargo. When it rains after midnight, the world
offers fragile wet kisses. Thank God
I put on a new roof, which I've enjoyed one year.

I say good-bye to that debt. Someone's car alarm
is threatened by this flood and so it's singing
in the fat dark. It's being turned off by a naked
neighbor. Books to pack, some to sell to

Twice-Loved Books on Market Street, no sweet
picnic in the pianissimo. New gutters

will prevent this Niagara Falls by my window.
The marijuana smokers on that third floor nest

across the street are awake; I pull down
the shades so they can continue to believe
they are alone. Who isn't alone tonight?
Russian Boris Slutsky (1919–86) writes:

"a sailor brings / Tattoos of purple to our landlocked
/ Landlubber's locality—" I open
the dictionary to the word *thrum*, tonight's
password. Perhaps Dante will bore me soon and

I can sleep, but no. Even Satan's asshole
is a spectacle. Rain slides off the letter V
upside down, the letter beloved by architects.
I'm sliding off my version of this world.

In Inferno, it rains sulfur—what a mess,
what shine. I go to sleep in this red city
by listening to the dark rain seek refuge
where it can, while the world isn't a dream.

Red

That history outside of color charts.
Many of us wear scars as if shrugs.

The red of a kiss, a mouth becoming
a month. Fire isn't shy except

when it is an idea. But *that* red.
What cools into a saint's eyeball,

what genitalia that comets wish
were theirs, what a volcano proves

is its thrust's last will and testament.
Red at home, kissing back. The opposite

of the moon. The red of a wound.
One mapped years later when a faint river.

The Quiet

Behold what quiet settles on the world.
—Vladimir Mayakowsky, "Past One O'clock"

Poets kill themselves because their art is
as much punctuation as it is vision:
the end the end the end. Sometimes I forget
none of this matters and that I shouldn't

worry about Yeats. He no longer paces
in his Tower, and that storm that makes him
write for his daughter is long over. Mami
bought me books never knowing how dangerous

they were. The burning of the library
of Alexandria was God's pyre.
Words sighed with relief, freed to copulate.
None shall see them in the act and live.

Write What You Know

But what do I know? I know Papi
worked in factories reigned by melodrama
(a sick day = the righteous anger of

waltzing bosses in K-Mart suits). I know
the word "knowledge" has the words
"now" and "ledge." I know that

my parents dared to color the suburbs
with their shy children. I'm no longer shy.
"Chew garlic," Mami said just yesterday after

I was diagnosed with pneumonia (I can't yet
breathe in the America I so love). I must write
about the time a museum guard yelled

at Papi: "The service entrance is over there."
Forgive me, Papi, for wanting to see dinosaurs.
(He's an aging man who abandoned me as an adult.)

Papi was silly, but he stopped dreaming
after citizen classes (but Puerto Ricans are
Americans I must still tell my frowning

scholarship geniuses). I know that Uncle
Manolo, who died in the green disgrace
of gangrene, did want to teach me the 12-string

guitar, but we visited less and less until
we were merely scars to each other, sad
genealogies. I know una tía became religious

decades after offering me a *Playboy* and
an egg timer. I know another tía talks
to spirits between epilepsy carnivals.

She is sweet and tough, what the grave
yearns for when thinking of honey.
I know that in poetry workshops I've lied:

"I'm not autobiographical." *They* don't need
to know Mami ripped a real blouse while
screaming at Heaven as if an eavesdropper

with a big diary. Papi's pornography was
disappointing because it wasn't imaginative.
I know I was judgmental, one way

to survive. I know that I miss feeding the camels
of the Three Wise Men. (Forget the presents—
camels in Chicago!) I know my teacher in

elementary school told me she was *glad* that
someday I'd be raped in prison. I know that
I've masturbated towards fake passports.

I've always loved details as if they are
sharable coins. I know that some colleagues
treating me to one dinner were naive in thinking

I knew the Mexican waiters who cursed them
every time they smiled under the parachutes of
fragile mustaches. We were and weren't strangers.

Will I get an award for knowing Mami hid her silver
Jack Kennedy dollars in the bathroom? I know God
has plans for me, but I'd rather do it myself, gracias.

I write without permission and no one knows how
often I'm rejected, and when I do publish, *they* smirk,
"Affirmative Action." My future is as an antique.

I know a man's morning beard can rub me raw
so that it feels that even sandpaper has a soul.
I know that I want to be known in my earned bed,

that it's worth it to be kept out of anthologies
because machos clone themselves without end.
My crotch has a mind of its own; I'm a double exile.

Sí, I know that none of this matters and yet
it hurts, it hurts. I know that once upon a time,
I used to be a brave little brown boy. The man I am

has memory losses that medicine can't help.
I know there are evil men trying to trade
new poems for old poems: newer, swifter,

correct models. I know that the writing
workshop is a minefield. I know that I cannot
stop writing, that the involuntary muscles

are in it for the long run. I know I must
write to scare myself. I know that my beloved
Hardy Boys may never recognize me

from other migrant workers while solving
The Mystery of the Lost Muchacho.
I'm waving to them: here I am, here I am.

Hombres, how many more clues do you need?

The Art of Money

after Yannis Ritsos

Clock radio's advice: *be rich*.
The kitchen's fresh paint doesn't

smell like *sea foam*. A pigeon passes
the hanging basket of oranges.

A bell is ringing. There isn't a church
nearby, nor an ice cream truck.

My body is warm. Unlike that statue of
the Irish immigrant I touched in

the Virgin Islands. Why ask for miracles
if you don't expect them, demand them?

You call out my nearest name, and
I whisper that Macedonia's new flag has

Alexander the Great's 13-pointed star.
Also, two dead *spinsters* were found

in a nearby trailer park. You sleep again.
Why can't rent be paid with poems?

Amateur Filmmaker

Close-up. I'm unshaven. It's OK, for I'm invisible in Chicago
tonight. My shadow wears a long coat borrowed from the black
moon.

I get seasick just riding Earth.
Today's happy hour is outside
of bars. Trees with thousands
of fingers tickle my silly shadow.
Downhill on Broadway. Gravity,
kiss me. Clouds weigh my eyelids.

.

From a locker room, I journey into the dark streets and pass
two generations of jazz players, and both are asking for the
same coin in my pocket. I ponder a liquor store's promise: "like
dying & going to Heaven."

Even the priests were naked in
that Catholic pool that was
surrounded by walls with peepholes.
I go down Argyle Street alone.
A human-size dragon drags New Year's
into an ancient New Chinatown.

.

I sit on my porch, my underwear glowing like a verb. My heart
refuses to sleep like the rest of Chicago. Lake Michigan looks
like a black eye.

Did gods make the stars from
the bones of dead sparrows?
Séance with Charles Darwin:
there's a monkey on the cross
and a smiling ape in my jock.
The moon cannot mirror my skull.

.

A ride on a subway train, heading towards Argyle Street. The
Chicago skyline is a white wall, trembling at the thought of graffiti.

A magician on the glowing train
can't stop touching himself everywhere:
a brief letter from you, love?
Sometimes I smell the olives from
the far garden of the Christ of my
hard childhood. Stop, this is my stop.

.

Along the black lake's edge I stumble and spy on fishermen and
drug traders, whose presence is revealed only by lit cigarettes,
tiny lighthouses.

It's always about loneliness, isn't it?
I'm teaching other people's children
while I have a cat misnamed as Destiny.
Today's horoscope was so mysterious.
I'm mistaking dreams for memories.
Is Judgment Day a big film festival?

That Flag

The Motel 6 clerk thinks I'm
Italian and complains to me
about Puerto Ricans, and I
nod because she has the key
to the last cheap room in town.
I unpack and go for a ride
down Joe Peréz Road and watch
two white, shirtless men do drug deals.
One looks at me, laughs. What does
he see? This sexy thug has
a Confederate flag in his truck
window. He rubs himself again
and again and I watch the way
one is possessed by a wreck.
The deal done, the two men then
slap each other on the ass,
and ride dust storms back to town.
I sit there thinking the fuckers
are right, that they are big
handsome, that they are our
America's perfect heirs and
that I'm not—aging Puerto Rican
homosexual poet exiled
to a borrowed bed. I walk
past the clerk and sing "Buenas
noches," but it isn't one, for I dream
of that flag, of a terrible army
of soldiers in uniforms of skin
sent to steal from me the head
of Joe Peréz. But I've hidden it
inside my own skull. It is safe.

75

♾This book is printed on acid-free, archival-quality paper.
Manufactured in the United States of America

Library of Congress Cataloging-in-Publication Data
Arroyo, Rane.
Home movies of Narcissus : poems / by Rane Arroyo.
p. cm. - (Camino del sol)
ISBN 0-8165-2195-6 (pbk. : alk. paper)
1. Hispanic Americans—Poetry.
2. Identity (Psychology)—Poetry.
I. Title. II. Series.
PS3551.R722 H66 2002
811'.54—dc21   2002001768

British Library Cataloguing-in-Publication Data
A catalogue record for this book is available from the British Library.

Publication of this book is made possible in part by the proceeds of a permanent
endowment created with the assistance of a Challenge Grant from the National
Endowment for the Humanities, a federal agency.

Rane Arroyo is a poet
and playwright
who has traveled the United States
but calls the Midwest home.
His Puerto Rican and gay cultures
have also influenced his work.
He is the author of three
previous books of poems:
*Columbus's Orphan, The Singing
Shark,* and *Pale Ramón.*
Arroyo has won many awards
and grants but confesses that
the Carl Sandburg Poetry Prize
is his favorite:
He won it in his hometown
on a birthday weekend,
and the award is named for
one of his dissertation figures.
He is currently a professor
at The University of Toledo,
where he is Director
of Creative Writing.